THE STUDY OF SCIENCE

Science

Its History and Development

Edited by Hope Lourie Killcoyne

Britannica
Educational Publishing

IN ASSOCIATION WITH

ROSEN
EDUCATIONAL SERVICES

Published in 2015 by Britannica Educational Publishing (a trademark of Encyclopædia Britannica, Inc.) in association with The Rosen Publishing Group, Inc.
29 East 21st Street, New York, NY 10010

Distributed exclusively by Rosen Publishing.
To see additional Britannica Educational Publishing titles, go to rosenpublishing.com

First Edition

Britannica Educational Publishing
J.E. Luebering: Director, Core Reference Group
Anthony L. Green: Editor, Compton's by Britannica

Rosen Publishing
Hope Lourie Killcoyne: Executive Editor
Intro and additional text by Daniel E. Harmon
Nelson Sá: Art Director
Michael Moy: Designer
Cindy Reiman: Photography Manager
Marty Levick: Photo Researcher

Library of Congress Cataloging-in-Publication Data

Science: its history and development/editor, Hope Lourie Killcoyne.—First edition.
        pages cm.—(The study of science)
Includes bibliographical references and index.
ISBN 978-1-62275-421-2 (library bound)
1. Science—History—Juvenile literature. I.Killcoyne, Hope Lourie, editor.
Q125.S385 2015
509—dc23

                                                                    2014004692

Manufactured in the United States of America

On the cover: *SuperStock/Getty Images; cover and interior pages borders and backgrounds © iStockphoto.com/ LuMaxArt*

CONTENTS

At first naturally fearful of fire, our ancestors in time learned to conquer, harness, and utilize fire to their advantage, marking one of the first scientific advances of humanity. Sheila Terry/Science Source

Armchair philosophers for hundreds of years have pondered a favorite question: What was the first scientific invention? Some say the knife. Some say the wheel, others the boat. Some say learning to start, use, and control fire. Whatever the correct answer—and whether it came about by accident or experimentation—it was the beginning of a long legacy of discovery resulting from human curiosity. It might be said that there have been "scientists" for as long as there have been people.

The story of science dates to long before the beginning of recorded history. Isaac Asimov, a famous science fiction and nonfiction author and biochemistry professor, suggested in one of his books that the first human scientific advance occurred four million years ago. It was when primitive humans became bipeds, rising to walk on two legs. Perhaps the next big thing scientifically—the use of stone tools—occurred two million years later. A million and a half years after that, archaeologists estimate, humans learned how to take advantage of fire

9

for warmth and cooking. Fire was a natural phenomenon they instinctively had feared for a very long time.

Ever so gradually, science advanced. Prehistoric men and women learned to cultivate crops, in addition to foraging for wild plants and hunting game. They developed wheels (most likely inspired by rolling logs) and adapted them for transporting heavy loads. They learned to count. They cut and shaped copper, tin, and other metals for many practical purposes, from coins to armor. They began to understand better ways to take advantage of and survive in the changing seasons. They learned that certain plant foods were nutritious and curative, others poisonous.

Dates and circumstances of the earliest scientific developments are unknown because the people who made them had no system of writing. What they learned was passed down to younger generations by word of mouth. Their findings were not entirely unrecorded, however. Prehistoric drawings in different parts of the world indicate how people lived. They show that certain early cultures had fairly advanced understandings of agriculture, celestial objects, and other complexities of the natural world.

With the advent of writing, experimenters and scribes began recording the history of scientific development. We know much, for example, of the work of ancient Chinese astronomer Zhang Heng, who studied the stars and invented a seismometer to detect earthquakes. We know that the mathematician Archimedes demonstrated the powers of the lever in classical Greece. We benefit from the extensive teachings of brilliant scientists of the Renaissance and more recent eras. Each step forward in modern times has been well chronicled. Today, we read regularly of breaking discoveries, from microbiology to deep space. Exciting research is constantly underway.

New fields of science have emerged as a result of new tools. The invention of the compound microscope in the late 16th century led to minute studies of organisms and substances. In recent years, advances in digital technology have provided far greater access to information and faster modes of communication.

In this book, we will trace the progression of science through its transition from "history" to "current events."

SCIENCE IN OUR WORLD

Humans incessantly explore, experiment, create, and examine the world. The active process by which physical, biological, and social phenomena are studied is known as science. Individuals involved in science, called

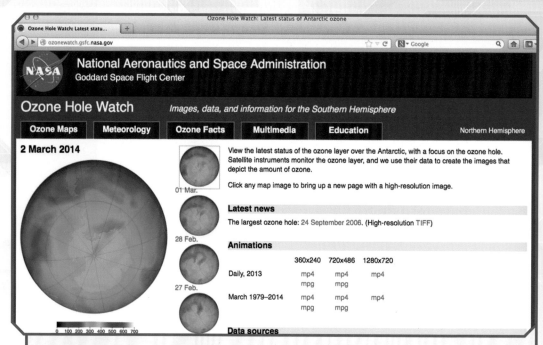

The National Aeronautics and Space Administration (NASA) keeps a close watch on the ozone layer in our atmosphere via satellite imagery, which it then color-codes. In this March 2014 view of the Antarctic pole, blue shows areas with the least ozone. NASA Ozone Watch

scientists, often spend their entire lives in pursuit of answers to probing questions. This ongoing process often leads to new areas of scientific inquiry.

Although many areas of scientific inquiry are interrelated, specific scientific disciplines, or divisions, have been established. The sciences can be broadly divided into two main areas: the natural sciences and the social sciences. The natural sciences comprise the physical sciences, earth and space sciences, and life sciences; the social sciences encompass disciplines that deal with social and cultural aspects of human behavior, such as economics, sociology, and psychology.

Some scientists are driven by little more than the desire to learn. They may study to gain knowledge for its own sake. These scientists are engaged in basic, or pure, science. Their projects may or may not have any relevance to everyday life. Scientists working in applied science, on the other hand, usually have a specific goal in mind. This goal may involve a product, process, business, or other human need. An applied scientist often uses information recently gathered by other scientists as well as the cumulative knowledge of the pure sciences.

THE SIGNIFICANCE OF SCIENCE IN SOCIETY

Science plays a major role in society, and even nonscientists can appreciate scientific progress. Because of science, human understanding of the past, present, and future is constantly in a state of flux. For instance, decades ago the notion of identifying the entire genetic code of an organism would have seemed an impossible feat. Today, it is a mark of scientific progress. Because scientific inquiry never ceases to exist, events once dismissed as material for science fiction, such as medical therapy based on an individual's genetic makeup, now seem inevitable.

Science technology can be found in nearly all aspects of everyday life. For instance, if electricity had never been discovered, electric appliances, heaters, and lights would not exist. Electronic components found in radios, television sets, laptop computers, and cellular telephones are now smaller and more reliable than before. Advances in electronics are responsible for what is called the digital age. Through computer technology, information can be processed and communicated globally in seconds.

At one time, computers were extremely expensive. They were rarely found outside of laboratories and large businesses. Since their manufacture is now economical, computers and computer-based devices have become very common. Computers are used not only in offices for all kinds of essential business functions and in schools and universities for study and research, they are also used in the home for communication, entertainment, and many other purposes. Many people carry portable computer-based cellular telephones. Computers help operate many processes and systems crucial to modern life, including electric power grids, communication networks, financial markets, and air-traffic control facilities.

In physics, the discovery and control of nuclear energy has had a tremendous effect on international relations and on the economies of many countries—in

The Apple iPad Mini is one of the growing array of tablet computers. Today a large variety of computers—used in offices, homes, parks, or about anywhere—provide a world of instantaneous information, entertainment, and communication to millions of users worldwide. Sean Gallup/Getty Images News/Thinkstock

STEM CELLS

There are hundreds of different types of cells in the human body. Most of them start out as stem cells. Stem cells contain the instructions needed to make the cell grow into a specialized type, such as a muscle, nerve, or blood cell. The ways that stem cells develop into specialized cells is not yet fully understood.

Scientists are working on the idea that a stem cell can be instructed to grow into a particular type of cell, such as a liver cell. If enough liver cells are grown to produce liver tissue that works normally, they could be transplanted into a person whose own liver has failed. This research could lead to treatments for many conditions and diseases, including Alzheimer's disease, Parkinson's disease, heart disease, diabetes, and damage to the spinal cord.

The most useful types of stem cells come from embryos (unborn babies that are still at a very early stage of development). Embryos are sometimes created in a laboratory as part of a process to help people have babies. Scientists can take cells called an egg from a woman and sperm from a man and combine them in the laboratory. The embryos that are created in this way can then be placed inside the woman's body to allow the baby to develop or they can be kept in the laboratory. Some of the embryos are donated for use in research. Scientists can also get embryonic stem cells by cloning, or copying, cells.

Some stem cells come from adults. But these cells are not as useful for research. They may not live as long, and they may not develop into as many types of tissue as embryonic stem cells. They are also harder to gather.

Many people are opposed to the use of stem cells from embryos on ethical grounds. They do not think that it is right to use embryos in this way. They see embryos as living human beings. They do not like the fact that the embryos are destroyed in the process of gathering the stem cells.

However, others say that the embryos used for such research come from people who want to donate them for research. They see the embryos as collections of cells, and they think that the research is important because it could help improve the lives of many people.

terms of the production of nuclear weapons as well as the use of nuclear energy for generating electricity for homes, businesses, and factories. Physicists once thought of the atom as the elementary building block of matter. Using particle accelerators, they later determined that the nuclei of atoms themselves are composed of many types of elementary particles that are held together by strong, short-range forces.

Physicists have also invented sophisticated lasers that produce concentrated beams of light. Lasers are used in medicine, industry, communications, navigation, and the military. Scientists working in the area of physical chemistry have produced materials called superconductors, which theoretically

can carry an electric current forever without electric power input. The first known superconductors operated only at very cold temperatures, but new classes of superconducting materials have been discovered that operate at warmer, though still very cold, temperatures. Superconductors are used in a variety of applications that require powerful electromagnets, including as particle accelerators, imaging devices, and laboratory equipment.

The battle against disease and illness has also gained much from science. Safer surgical procedures are now in use, including those for organ transplantation and coronary bypass surgery. Many procedures have been improved because of the development of specialized medical instruments. Some instruments enable physicians to see inside the body without making a single incision. Others can carry out essential bodily functions, such as pumping blood or breathing. Medical research has led to the development of vaccinations and pharmaceutical drugs to prevent or treat many life-threatening diseases and disorders. A new focus of research is to seek a better understanding of stem cells for potential medical applications.

Some scientific and technological advances have the potential to alter the environment significantly. The release of certain synthetic chemical compounds into the air can cause undesirable atmospheric changes, such as the destruction of the ozone layer. Damage to the ozone layer would allow increased amounts of ultraviolet radiation from the Sun to penetrate the atmosphere and cause a large increase in the rate of skin cancer. The burning of fossil fuels releases into the atmosphere large amounts of carbon dioxide, which has the effect of trapping the Sun's heat—the greenhouse effect. With an ongoing increase in the global average temperature of the atmosphere, it is feared that climates in many regions of the world will change and that ice sheets in the Arctic and Antarctic will melt. The melting ice would lead to a higher sea level and cause flooding in coastal areas. In order to gain further information about these potentially dangerous developments, scientists monitor the ozone layer and atmospheric carbon dioxide, and they study the complex interaction of solar radiation, the atmosphere, and Earth's surface.

Another mark of scientific advancement is the improved understanding of the world's

Wind farms can be a valuable source of electric power in places where the climate is favorable.
Stephen Meese/Shutterstock.com

limited supply of petroleum. Concerns about the world's future energy needs have resulted in the study of alternative energy resources, which include solar energy, nuclear energy, wind energy, wave energy, and energy from Earth's own internal heat.

THE SCIENTIFIC METHOD

Scientifically minded people generally believe in cause-and-effect relationships. They feel there is a perfectly natural explanation for most things. For example, there is a reason why milk sours and why some leaves turn red in the fall, while others turn yellow. Changes such as these, which are easily observed, are known as phenomena. Some common phenomena are not completely understood. Still others cannot be explained at all at this time. The belief that effects have causes plays a significant part in scientific inquiry. The cause of AIDS, for example, was once unknown. Nevertheless, scientists firmly believed that a cause existed. Once they discovered that AIDS was caused by a virus, scientists could search for a remedy such as a vaccine. If everyone believed that a disease just happened without a natural cause, no progress would be made in learning to control it.

Scientists spend tremendous amounts of time making observations and gathering information, or data. They may work individually or as part of a team to learn what they can about a specific problem or an unexplained phenomenon. Problems or questions of interest for investigation have a variety of sources. Sometimes they arise from curiosity following a chance observation. Awareness may also result from reading, from earlier laboratory experiments, from discussions with colleagues, from practical problems to be

solved, or simply from thinking. Sometimes new information or discoveries require verifying previous investigations.

The formal model for a scientific investigation consists of a series of steps called the scientific method. According to this model, a scientist first identifies a question that can be investigated and then tries to learn as much as possible about it. Frequently this involves studying books and journals that contain information about the question, a procedure known as searching the literature. The scientist thinks of a possible answer or explanation (called a hypothesis) to the question under study and then designs an experiment to test the hypothesis. The results of the experiment are compared to the expected results, which will either suggest that the hypothesis is accurate or that it needs to be revised. Once the hypothesis is revised and retested as necessary, the scientist reports the results and the hypothesis may gain the acceptance of other scientists.

Although scientific reports are often presented in terms of the scientific method, the way in which scientific inquiries proceed in practice is not fixed, and they may follow a variety of unexpected paths. Science is a process of discovery that involves testing ideas and communicating with others. It may yield knowledge, provide solutions to problems, or inform public policy. Testing ideas involves interpreting gathered data and observations. Sometimes experiments do not produce usable results but lead to new avenues of investigation.

Testing hypotheses is an important way for scientists to gather data to develop, support, or challenge scientific theories. A scientific theory is an explanation of an observation or a natural phenomenon and is based on and supported by a large body of evidence. Most scientific theories have been so well tested that they are generally accepted with confidence and are unlikely to be further tested. For example, the heliocentric theory explains that Earth revolves around the Sun. Although it was greatly challenged when first proposed by Nicolaus Copernicus, this theory is well supported by evidence and unlikely to be challenged today. However, some theories, though widely accepted—such as the theory of evolution by natural selection—are occasionally challenged through new hypotheses and subsequent testing.

PHILOSOPHY OF SCIENCE

Humans have always been curious about their surroundings. One of the most fundamental

quests is the explanation of human origin and destiny. Perhaps this is where natural philosophy begins—in the search for the relationship between humans and the universe. All societies have tried to explain the origin of humans and their role in nature. These questions have been addressed by philosophers, religious scholars, and scientists alike.

Religion has had a tremendous influence on the discoveries and opinions of the scientific community. The Italian natural philosopher Galileo Galilei, for example, had tremendous difficulty convincing the Roman Catholic Church of the truth of his astronomical findings. His idea of a Sun-centered (heliocentric) solar system contradicted the Earth-centered (geocentric) model accepted by the church. He was put on trial for sharing his observations, and he spent parts of his life under close supervision because of his ideas. Another historic controversy centers on the age of Earth. Some religious traditions set Earth's age at about 6,000 years. However, scientists believe Earth is much older—about 4.5 billion years old. In both examples, science and religion have differed in the way they gather information about the world.

Throughout modern history, science and religion have often been portrayed as

Italian astronomer and physicist Galileo standing before the Papal Tribunal, by which he was tried for heresy for espousing a heliocentric model of the solar system. In 1992, more than 350 years after the 1633 trial pictured above, the Italian scientist was pardoned by Pope John Paul II and the church finally accepted his teachings. Time & LIfe Pictures/Getty Images

irreconcilable opponents, continually locked in a struggle over the meaning of truth. Scientists themselves are often characterized as fundamentally antireligious or atheistic. In 1916, a survey of 1,000 scientists and mathematicians, in which they were questioned regarding their religious beliefs, revealed that roughly 40 percent of respondents believed in a god who communicated to humankind and to whom it was possible to pray "in expectation of receiving an answer." Forty-five percent of the respondents stated that they did not

believe in a god as defined in the survey, and 15 percent answered that they were either agnostic or did not have a definite opinion on the question. In 1997, the same survey was conducted again, and the results nearly mirrored those of 81 years earlier. The only large variation in the 1997 results came from those respondents who did not believe in a god as defined by the questionnaire—3 percent more scientists felt this way in 1997. In both surveys, approximately 400 of the scientists who received the questionnaires did not respond. The results of the survey seemed to debunk the general caricatures of scientific intolerance for religion.

Like philosophy, science emphasizes the use of logic. In fact, science can be viewed as a scrutinizing system of logic. It seeks to answer questions by observing phenomena. As scientists try to solve a problem, they may use a model based on a logical, plausible connection of events. Like a hypothesis, the model is then tested by making predictions based on the model. If the predictions are proven wrong, then the model is revised. If the model survives the tests, the model becomes the system of logic that describes the theory. Theoretical models of this nature have been used to study economics, the structure of the atom, the universe, evolution, and even the origin of life.

Unlike philosophy, science emphasizes the repeatability of results. This means that a given set of circumstances should always produce the same result. Scientific theories are not accepted by the scientific community until they have been validated. One way to validate a theory is to have scientists in other laboratories duplicate the experiment or the calculations. Using another set of materials and methods, these scientists may repeat the experiment and check the accuracy of the previous report. This long and careful process will confirm that the original result was not merely a fluke occurrence, a misinterpretation of events, or an error in procedure.

By having several scientists investigate a situation, the most accurate description of cause and effect can be determined. Many of the most basic questions in science can be phrased in the form: "How does…?", "Why does…?", and "What determines…?" These are all attempts to establish cause and effect. A difficulty arises when many factors, or variables, affect the system at one time. A variable is something that has different values under different conditions. In one type of laboratory test all the variables but one are controlled. The uncontrolled variable is known as the

experimental variable, and the others are the control variables. This method of testing is called controlled experimentation.

FIRE: ONE OF THE EARLIEST DISCOVERIES

Science was unknown for thousands of years before the dawn of recorded history. Nevertheless, many significant discoveries and inventions were made during this pre-scient time. One of these discoveries was that fire could be harnessed and put to work.

While some animals have an instinctive fear of fire, humans somehow discovered that fire could be controlled and kept in one place. No one knows exactly when this discovery was first made. However, archaeologists have found that during the Ice Age humans used fire for cooking and to keep warm. Today, this very same source of heat is used to produce steam for turbines.

EARLY HUNTING METHODS AND AGRICULTURE

Early humans also used fire to help hunt and kill animals for food. One method used, called the fire drive, enabled a few people to kill several animals without a great deal of work.

First, animals had to be found grazing near a cliff during the summer when grass was dry. Then, when the wind was blowing in the right direction, a few hunters set fire to the dry grass with torches. The flames drove the animals over the cliff. By using fire in this way, early hunters had more to eat after a small amount of work than they would have had after a full week of hunting with a spear or club.

For a long time humans roamed across the land hunting wild animals for food. Eventually, doglike creatures were noticed to have an instinctive ability to detect game even when the hunters could not see it. These creatures often followed the hunters, and they were gradually trained to find game for the hunters to kill. Then dog and hunter would share the spoils of the hunt. In time humans realized that other wild animals could also be domesticated and kept for human use. They also found that they did not have to travel great distances to gather edible plants. Plants could be grown where they were needed. Soon humans began to raise crops.

OTHER EARLY DISCOVERIES

Primitive methods of tanning leather and weaving were discovered by about 5000 BCE.

Humans also learned how to make clay pots in which to store things. Perhaps the accidental exposure of such a pot to a fire resulted in the first pottery. These clay pots could not be used for cooking, however, because clay, whether burned or not, is a poor conductor of heat. Instead, round stones were put in an open fire. When they were red hot, they were scooped up with a wooden or clay ladle and dumped into a pot of water. The stones would then heat the water and cook the food. This ancient method of cooking was still used in some areas until the beginning of the 20th century.

Another early invention was the wheel. The inspiration for the wheel may have come from using logs as rollers to move heavy objects. Whatever the origin, the wheel was readily adapted to a variety of uses. Placed horizontally, a wheel was an aid in making pottery, though its greatest value was its use on primitive carts for carrying heavy loads. Waterwheels were devised as tools for lifting water, and windmills became power sources.

One of the first metals put to use by early humans was copper. Like gold and silver, this metal is sometimes found in nature in pure form. Since it is so malleable, it can also be hammered into various shapes without first

A large clay pot believed to be from the 6th century BCE. *The artifact was discovered in the Marche region along Italy's Adriatic coast, once known as the ancient region of Picenum.* DEA/A. Dagli Orti/De Agostini/Getty Images

being heated. The discovery of how to heat ore and smelt metals was probably made by accident. A mixture of tin and copper yields bronze, which came to be widely used.

Having learned that ores could be smelted, humans probably tried the process on many different substances. Often the work was wasted, but occasionally the result was useful. Glass was possibly discovered in this way.

Soon after the smelting of metals became common, metal money was probably invented. Pieces of money with a fixed value made trade and commerce possible. Copper was used for the least valuable pieces, silver for the more valuable coins, and gold for the most valuable.

THE BEGINNING OF WRITING

Writing began in Mesopotamia and Egypt several thousand years before the start of the Common Era. Picture writing was probably the first method of setting down what people saw, heard, or felt. This was called pictographic writing. It was many centuries before any kind of alphabet was developed.

Ancient Egyptian hieroglyphics—characters of a writing system that uses pictures and symbols—appear on a wall of the great temple at Karnak, Egypt. Donya Nedomam/ Shutterstock.com

By the time writing began, all the above-mentioned discoveries and many more had been made. Their use, however, was not scientific. The tanner, for example, did not really know what happened chemically to a piece of animal skin that he converted into useful leather. His knowledge of the tanner's art had simply been learned from his elders. He knew what to do but not why it worked. Glassmakers and those who smelted metals had no knowledge of the chemistry involved in the processes they used. This was true of artisans of all kinds. They were highly skilled at their crafts, but they had no idea of the scientific principles involved.

Writing made possible the beginning of science. It enabled humans to record what one generation of people had learned and to pass it on to the people of the next generation. There were no formalized sciences such as geography, zoology, or botany then. The ancients, however, did describe and list the names of places, animals, and plants.

THE BEGINNINGS OF SCIENCE IN GREECE

The first sciences in the modern sense were those connected with mathematics.

They were begun in Mesopotamia and in ancient Egypt and were passed on to ancient Greece.

Mathematics and mechanics were put to practical use during the Golden Age of Greece, beginning about 600 BCE. The knowledge of geometry was applied widely in Greek architecture. The Greek philosopher Archimedes was a great mathematician and an important early writer on the science of mechanics. The knowledge of physics was used in building as well as in war. The lever made it possible to move huge stones for building. With the catapult soldiers were able to hurl heavy spears or large rocks at enemy fortifications.

Another science that the ancient Greeks developed was astronomy. They could foretell to the day when a given planet would

Archimedes, who lived in the 3rd century BCE, was both mathematician and scientist. His careful calculations and study of mechanics made him a pioneer of physics. Leemage/ Universal Images Goup/Getty Images

ARCHIMEDES

The first scientist to recognize and use the power of the lever was Archimedes (287–212 BCE). This gifted Greek mathematician and inventor once said, "Give me a place to stand and rest my lever on, and I can move the Earth." He also invented the compound pulley and Archimedes' screw. Archimedes was a brilliant mathematician who helped develop the science of geometry. He discovered the relation between the surface area and volume of a sphere and those of its circumscribing cylinder.

A legend says that Archimedes discovered the principle of displacement while stepping into a full bath. He realized that the water that ran over equaled in volume the submerged part of his body. Through further experiments, he deduced the principle of buoyancy, which is called Archimedes' principle. According to this principle a body immersed in a fluid loses as much in weight as the weight of an equal volume of the fluid.

Another legend describes how Archimedes uncovered a fraud against King Hieron II of Syracuse using his principle of buoyancy. The king suspected that a solid gold crown he ordered was partly made of silver. Archimedes first took two equal weights of gold and silver and compared their weights when immersed in water. Next he compared the weights of the crown and a pure silver crown of identical dimensions when each was immersed in water. The difference between these two comparisons revealed that the crown was not solid gold.

Archimedes was born in Syracuse, Sicily. He lived there most of his life. When the Romans attacked Syracuse, Archimedes invented weapons to defend the city. He is said to have suggested a method of employing mirrors to set enemy ships afire. After a two-year siege the Romans finally entered the city, and Archimedes was killed in the battle that followed.

be visible and even where it would appear in the heavens. This kind of science was what would be known today as the "astronomy of position."

Theoretical science began when the Greeks started to ask serious questions about the world around them. They wanted to know what things were made of and where they came from. They wished not only to make and build things but to know how and why things were as they were. Asking these questions and getting the first answers—many of which were later proved wrong—laid the foundations of Western science. The Greeks passed their theories on to the Romans and the other people of western Europe. For many centuries European science was based for the most part on the early theories of the Greeks.

37

THE ROMAN EMPIRE

The Romans widened the range of practical science. Their road-building feats were not equaled until modern times. They made the first road maps, with distances between stations along their roads carefully measured in paces. They built great aqueducts to carry water over long distances.

THE DARK AGES AND THE MIDDLE AGES

The period from the end of the Roman Empire to about 800 CE is often called the Dark Ages. There was not much progress made in Europe during this period. The foundations were laid, however, for important advances that were to follow in the later Middle Ages and the Renaissance.

The stirrup was probably invented during the Dark Ages. Waterwheels also made their first appearance then. They were used as sources of power in small rivers and in sea inlets, where they were run by tidal currents. The waterwheel led to the windmill, which was introduced about 1100. The magnetic compass was also invented about this time.

PAPERMAKING AND FIREARMS

By the 13th century papermaking spread throughout Europe. Paper was a Chinese invention. It had been adopted by the Persians and then by the Arabs, who brought the art to Europe.

Powder (not gunpowder, because guns were not yet known) and fireworks rockets were introduced into Europe in the 1200s. They had been invented in China some years earlier.

The earliest mention of firearms is in a Dutch chronicle dated 1313. It states that

Armed forces of the Holy Roman Emperor Maximilian I put a city under siege in about 1517. The use of a cannon represents a heavy artillery barrage, an early version of today's ballistic missiles. Graphische Sammlung Albertina, Vienna, Austria/The Bridgeman Art Library

firearms were invented in Germany. The first picture of a primitive cannon can be found in an English manuscript dated 1326.

GUTENBERG'S CONTRIBUTION

In the 15th century Johannes Gutenberg developed a practical method of printing. The Chinese had invented movable type in the 11th century but made little use of it. Gutenberg's printing method started a new era in the growth of science.

Before Gutenberg, a student might spend a whole year copying a book by hand. After Gutenberg, books were printed much more quickly. They were also available in large enough quantities for universities to expand their libraries for the increased use of both faculty and students.

It was due mainly to the existence of the printed book that the great scientists of the 16th century could work systematically. Books made both old and new knowledge readily available. Anybody who truly wanted to learn could now do so because books could be easily circulated from person to person.

In spite of the rather large number of books that were written and printed in the 16th century, most of the sciences remained in their earliest stage. This earliest stage was the collection of everything that was known in a certain field, then the reviewing of that material or commenting on it. It did not include an explanation of why things were the way they were.

Andreas Vesalius, for example, did pioneer work in anatomy. He named every bone and muscle and most of the blood vessels in the body. He did not know, however, how the human body functioned. Zoologist Conrad Gesner listed all known animals, but he had no idea of the relationships of the various animals to one another. Georgius Agricola (Georg Bauer) wrote about the mining of metals and the processing of ores, but he knew nothing about chemistry. Gunnery master Leonhart Fronsperger wrote a book on guns and shooting, but he knew nothing of ballistics.

Flemish physician and surgeon Andreas Vesalius laid the foundations of modern anatomy. The woodcut, depicting Vesalius teaching anatomy, is the title page from the first edition of Seven Books on the Structure of the Human Body, *published in Latin in 1543.* Private Collection/Photo © Christie's Images/The Bridgeman Art Library

THE BREAKTHROUGH IN ASTRONOMY

In 1543 a historic book on astronomy was published. It was *Concerning the Revolutions of the Celestial Spheres* by Nicolaus Copernicus. For centuries the science of astronomy had been based on Ptolemaic theory that Earth was the center of the universe and motionless. The problem was to explain how the other planets and heavenly bodies moved.

At first it was thought that they simply moved in circular orbits around Earth. Calculations based on this view, however, did not agree with actual observations. Then it was thought that the other planets traveled in small circular orbits. These in turn were believed to move along larger orbits around Earth. With this

Nicolaus Copernicus. Leemage/Universal Images Group/Getty Images

NICOLAUS COPERNICUS

Nicolaus Copernicus (1473–1543) is often considered the founder of modern astronomy. His study led to the theory that Earth and the other planets revolve around the Sun.

Copernicus was born February 19, 1473, in Torun, Poland. After the death of his father, a wealthy merchant, the boy was reared by an uncle who sent him to the University of Kraków. There he studied liberal arts, including astronomy and astrology. Copernicus also studied law at Bologna and medicine at Padua in Italy. He became an officer in the Roman Catholic Church and lectured on mathematics in Rome. He returned to Poland in 1507 to attend to his elderly uncle. Copernicus spent his spare time studying the heavens.

Until then, astronomy was based on the ancient astronomer Ptolemy's theory that Earth was the center of the universe. Astronomers believed that the other planets and heavenly bodies orbited Earth. Copernicus's revolutionary idea was that Earth was one of the planets that revolved around the Sun. He also believed Earth rotated on an axis.

For years, he delayed publication of his controversial findings, which contradicted all the authorities of the time. The historic book that contains the final version of his theory, *De revolutionibus orbium coelestium libri vi* ("Six Books Concerning the Revolutions of the Celestial Spheres"), was not printed until 1543, the year of his death.

The book opened the way to a truly scientific approach to astronomy. It profoundly influenced later scientific thinkers such as Galileo, Johannes Kepler, and Isaac Newton.

theory, however, it could not be proved that Earth was the center of the universe.

In his historic book Copernicus said that the Earth should be regarded as one of the planets that revolved around the Sun. He also stated that the Earth rotated on an axis. Copernicus's theory, however, did not offer an adequate explanation of the movement of the planets. This explanation came more than a half century later.

Johannes Kepler. Science & Society Picture Library/Getty Images

KEPLER'S LAWS OF PLANETARY MOTION

Johannes Kepler spent years trying to work out the orbit of the planet Mars by means of a small circle (epicycle) moving along a larger one around the Sun. No matter how he tried, it did not work. Finally, he came

JOHANNES KEPLER

Johannes Kepler (1571–1630) is best known for his discovery that the orbits in which Earth and the other planets travel around the Sun are elliptical, or oval, in shape. He was also the first to explain correctly how human beings see and to demonstrate what happens to light when it enters a telescope. He designed an instrument that serves as the basis of the modern refractive telescope.

Kepler was born December 27, 1571, at Weil der Stadt in Germany. He was a sickly child but had a brilliant mind. After studying at the University of Tübingen, he taught astronomy and mathematics.

By Kepler's time, many astronomers had accepted that the Sun was the center of the solar system and that Earth turned on its axis, but they still believed the planets moved in circular orbits. Because of this, they could not explain the motions of the planets as seen from Earth. Kepler suspected the explanation was that the planetary orbits took a different shape. After six years, hampered by poor eyesight and the clumsy mathematical methods of the day, he found the answer: Mars follows an elliptical orbit at varying speeds.

In 1609, he published a book on the results of his work, *The New Astronomy*. He later wrote an important book on optics.

to realize that the movement of Mars could be understood. To do this one had to assume that the planet moved along an elliptical (oval) orbit at a speed that varied according to the planet's distance from the Sun.

Italian philosopher, astronomer, and mathematician Galileo, shown in a mezzotint from 1852 by Samuel Sartain, has been called the founder of modern science. Born in 1564, he was one of the first people to examine the heavens with a telescope. He also made breakthrough discoveries in the study of motion. Science Source/Photo Researchers/Getty Images

GALILEO'S WORK WITH THE TELESCOPE

While Kepler was working out his laws of planetary motion, Galileo Galilei proved that Copernicus was right in stating that Earth moved on its axis. He did this using a telescope.

Galileo had heard that Hans Lippershey, a Dutch maker of eyeglasses, had invented a tube that made distant things look near. Although Galileo knew very little about this primitive telescope, he made one himself. Using it, he discovered that the planet Jupiter had moons (satellites). He also saw that the planet Venus passed through phases as does Earth's Moon. This indicated Venus moves around the Sun inside Earth's orbit. He saw, too, that the Milky Way was made up of countless distant stars. Galileo's observations led him to conclude that Copernicus had been right in at least part of his theories regarding astronomy.

NEWTON'S DISCOVERIES

Kepler had been able to show how a planet moves. Later in the 17th century Sir Isaac Newton showed why it travels the way it does. Kepler wondered where the force to move a planet came from. Having found that the motion of the planet was faster near the Sun, he had speculated that

A 19th-century engraving depicts English physicist and mathematician Isaac Newton dispersing sunlight through a prism for a study of optics. Newton changed the course of physics and had an impact on all branches of knowledge. Print Collector/Hulton Archive/Getty Images

the driving force might come from the Sun. Newton showed that there was such a force and that its strength was inversely proportional to the square of a planet's distance from the Sun. In his book *Principia*, which appeared in 1687, Newton set forth three basic laws of motion and described the gravitational attraction between bodies. The laws of motion and gravitational attraction apply not only to the Sun and the planets but also to the motion of satellites in orbit and the flight of a rocket in the vacuum of space.

CHAPTER 4

SCIENCE IN THE 18TH AND 19TH CENTURIES

While Copernicus, Kepler, Galileo, and Newton were establishing astronomy as a science, material for other sciences was still just being accumulated.

ELECTRICITY

Strides were being made in other areas, for example by Otto von Guericke of Magdeburg, Germany, who invented a primitive way of making electricity. He took an ordinary grindstone and substituted a ball of sulfur for the stone. With one hand, he cranked the ball. With the other, he rubbed it. The friction created static electricity. Wax and amber balls were also used. Newton improved upon

Otto von Guericke. The German physicist was also an engineer, a natural philosopher, and the inventor of the first air pump. Hulton Archive/Getty Images

this method by substituting a glass ball for one of sulfur.

In 1729, Stephen Gray in England discovered that electricity could be conducted through metal rods. At this point the knowledge of electricity stopped growing because of some mistaken ideas about it.

The substances that could be used to produce electricity—sulfur, glass, wax, and amber—were called "electrics." They could be used to produce electricity, but they would not conduct it. The metal conductors that Gray had discovered would conduct electricity, but they could not produce it.

It was now reasoned that a substance had to be an "electric" or a "conductor." The proper distinction, of course, would have been "insulators" and "conductors," and a conductor could be used to produce electricity if it was insulated.

MATHEMATICS

Two very important mathematical developments took place during the 17th century. In 1614, John Napier invented logarithms. It had been possible to do long multiplication and division problems before the invention of logarithms. With logarithms, up to 90 percent of

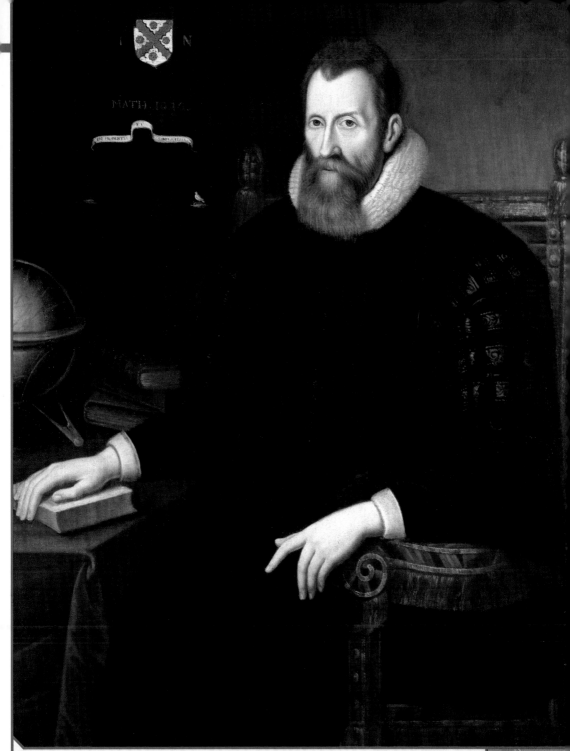

Scottish mathematician and theological writer John Napier, as depicted in a 1616 oil painting. Napier originated the concept of logarithms as a mathematical device to aid in calculations. Iberfoto/SuperStock

the time required for a given calculation could be saved.

Near the end of the 17th century, Newton in England and Gottfried Wilhelm von Leibniz in Germany were key figures in the development of calculus. Logarithms were mostly timesavers. Calculus is an important tool in solving a variety of complex problems commonly encountered in scientific fields.

THE STEAM ENGINE

The 18th century saw the development of a practical device as important and far-reaching in its results as the invention of movable type. This was the steam engine, a device as interesting for physics as it was useful for industry.

In order to understand the importance of the steam engine, it is necessary to understand an engineering term. The term is "firm power," which means simply power when and where it is wanted. A large windmill can be quite powerful, but it provides force only if wind happens to be blowing. A waterwheel comes closer to supplying firm power, but there is little choice in its location.

The steam engine provided firm power. It could be built anywhere. The only problem might be the transportation of fuel to make it run.

EARLY STEAM ENGINES

The earliest known form of steam engine was the machine built by Hero of Alexandria in the 1st century CE. This device was called an aeolipile, and it worked on the same principle as a lawn sprinkler, using steam rather than water. In 1629 Giovanni Branca invented the steam turbine. It worked by blowing a jet of steam against a kind of modified waterwheel. Neither of these machines was powerful enough to do any useful work.

The first useful steam engine was invented by Thomas Savery in 1698. It was known as a pumping engine because it had been invented for the specific purpose of pumping water from mine shafts. In this engine the hose, which was to suck up the water, led into a large container that had just been filled with steam. Then the steam valve was closed and a stream of cold water was run onto the metal container. The steam inside condensed. This produced a partial vacuum, and water was sucked into the container. The water was then drained from it.

Model of a Newcomen steam engine. Science & Society Picture Library/Getty Images

In 1705 Thomas Newcomen produced an "atmospheric engine," which had a piston connected to a large crossbeam. Steam was put into the cylinder to raise the piston. Next, cold water was sprayed into the cylinder, condensing the steam. The pressure of the atmosphere then forced the piston down. The piston, in turn, pulled down one end of the beam. The other end of the beam moved up at the same time. The crossbeam was used to drive a pump.

About 1760, James Watt of Scotland was asked to repair one of these atmospheric engines. He decided that cooling the cylinder after each stroke of the piston resulted in a waste of fuel. He tried to make the steam do the work directly without any cooling of the cylinder. His efforts resulted in the creation of an improved version of the engine in 1765.

THE BIOLOGICAL SCIENCES

Much of the progress in the biological sciences during the 18th century was due to the work of the Swedish botanist Carolus Linnaeus. Linnaeus had observed that some plants were quite similar while others were not. He established ways and means of fixing and describing plant similarities. Gradually, he constructed a botanical system

Carolus Linnaeus. Photo Researchers/ Getty Images

of classification in which he grouped like species into a genus, genera into orders, and orders into classes.

Linnaeus constructed a similar system for animals. After Linnaeus, a zoological catalogue was no longer merely a drawer of index cards with animals' names on them. There was now a zoological system. Students could see which animals were grouped together and how closely they were related.

CHEMISTRY

Important advances in the study of chemistry were made in the late 18th century. It is often said that chemistry grew out of alchemy. The alchemists had very special goals. They wanted to find something called the philosopher's stone or the elixir of life. With the help of these substances, they hoped to make gold from base metals and to cure all human ills. While the alchemists worked hard, it is unlikely that their efforts led to even a single great discovery.

Chemistry primarily grew out of the needs of smelters, metalworkers, tanners, dyers, and glassmakers. In the course of their work, new elements such as cobalt and nickel were discovered. Then, in the late 1700s, another element, oxygen, was discovered by Joseph Priestley and Carl Wilhelm Scheele.

THE PHLOGISTON THEORY

Many years before the discovery of oxygen, the growth of chemistry had been held back by a false theory regarding burning (combustion). Johann Becher and Georg Ernst Stahl tried to explain combustion by the phlogiston theory. According to this theory anything that could be burned contained an "essence" called phlogiston. When the substance burned, the phlogiston escaped into the air.

It had been observed that a substance would not burn long in a closed container. Becher and Stahl thought that combustion stopped because the air in the closed container

had become so saturated with phlogiston that it could not absorb any more of it. Today, of course, it is known that a substance burning in a closed container will stop burning when it uses up all the oxygen.

When oxygen was discovered, it was found that combustible substances burned much better in it than they did in air. It was then mistakenly assumed that oxygen had to be a gas completely devoid of phlogiston so that it could absorb whatever was released from the burning substance. The newly discovered oxygen was thus called "dephlogisticated air."

LAVOISIER'S CONTRIBUTION

When a metal is heated in air, an oxide is normally produced. The chemists of the 18th century called the oxide of a metal its calx. They reasoned that calx and the phlogiston together equaled the metal. The problem, however, was that the metal weighed less than its calx. The scientists of that period then further reasoned that since a substance became lighter by the addition of phlogiston, the phlogiston must therefore have a negative weight.

Thinking along this line became more and more confused. Finally the great French chemist Antoine-Laurent Lavoisier proved,

Antoine-Laurent Lavoisier conducting an experiment to determine the composition of water; from a 19th-century French engraving. Lavoisier is regarded as the founder of modern chemistry. Science Source/Photo Researchers/Getty Images

in 1783, that the metals were elements. He also showed that their so-called calxes (oxides) were the result of a combination of the metal and oxygen. At last freed from its self-made errors, chemistry progressed at a surprising rate.

ELECTRIC CURRENT

Just before the end of the 18th century, electric current was discovered. In 1780, an Italian named Luigi Galvani noticed that the legs of freshly killed frogs sometimes jerked when they touched metal. He thought this was caused by a kind of "animal electricity." Another Italian, Count Alessandro Volta, believed chemistry was involved. In 1800, Volta proved his theory when he built a primitive electric battery. This was called a voltaic cell.

By the end of the 18th century, the foundations for most of today's sciences had thus been laid. In chemistry, it was known what substances were the elements and what other substances were the compounds. In physics, the distinction between static electricity and electric (galvanic) current had been established. Astronomy had a firm foundation of theory.

ANTOINE-LAURENT LAVOISIER

One of the most honored scientists in history is Antoine-Laurent Lavoisier (1743–94). By revealing the truth about fire and burning, Lavoisier helped chemistry make its remarkable advance from that time on.

Lavoisier was born in Paris, France, on August 26, 1743. His wealthy father bought a title of nobility and wanted an aristocratic career for the boy. Young Lavoisier preferred science, however, so his father sent him to distinguished scholars. He studied mathematics, botany, and other sciences.

In 1768, he was elected to the Academy of Sciences. The same year he was appointed to the *ferme générale*, a body of men who held the right to "farm" (collect) taxes. In 1776, he became director of the government arsenal.

By 1783, Lavoisier had solved what was the most significant chemical problem of the day, showing the connection between oxygen and fire. Lavoisier proved that burning, the rusting of metals, and the breathing of animals all consist of the union of oxygen with other chemicals—oxidation, one of the most important chemical processes.

Lavoisier became commissioner of weights and measures and a commissary of the treasury. In 1794, however, French revolutionists accused him and other members of the *ferme générale* of plotting to cheat the government. He was executed in Paris by the revolutionary tribunal.

19TH–CENTURY GROWTH OF SCIENCE

Great scientific progress was made in the 19th century. This progress resulted from the application of what was already known, plus new discoveries of a basic nature. The steam engine in time became powerful enough to be used in ships and locomotives. The voltaic cell and thin metal rods, long known to conduct electricity, were developed into the electric telegraph.

In 1817, Swedish chemist Baron Jöns Jacob Berzelius realized that a substance he had thought to be tellurium was something else. He named his new substance selenium. Later it was discovered that when selenium was in the light, it would conduct an electric current. It would not, however, conduct a current in the dark.

One form of the early telephone developed from this property of selenium. It also resulted in experiments that finally led to "talking pictures," the transmission of pictures by wire, television, and the photoelectric cell, or electric eye.

In the mid-1800s, Gregor Mendel, an Austrian monk, made a significant discovery in biology. He found patterns of inheritance between parent plants and their offspring, and he proposed that certain plant characteristics could be inherited. This was the beginning of the study of genetics.

In the 16th century, Conrad Gesner collected all the information about animals available at that time. Later, Carolus Linnaeus compiled this information into a system that showed relationships among living things. Based on observations and descriptions of plants and animals, many of which were sent to him from the Americas, he categorized life into groups. The most closely related group, known as species, consisted of organisms that are capable of reproducing to form viable, healthy offspring in nature. Based on structure and appearance, living things are now classified according to their domain, kingdom, phylum, class, order, family, genus, and species.

Scientists then began wondering why species, though similar, still had slight variations. Naturalists such as Charles Darwin and Jean-Baptiste Lamarck sought to explain the seemingly perfect relationship between animals' habitat and their biological adaptations. Darwin developed his theory of organic evolution to explain these relationships. He

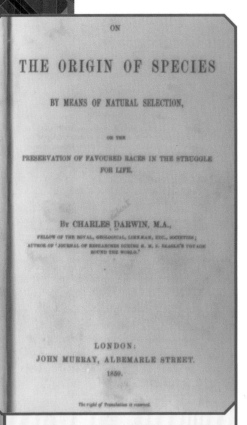

ON

THE ORIGIN OF SPECIES

BY MEANS OF NATURAL SELECTION,

OR THE

PRESERVATION OF FAVOURED RACES IN THE STRUGGLE
FOR LIFE.

By CHARLES DARWIN, M.A.,

FELLOW OF THE ROYAL, GEOLOGICAL, LINNEAN, ETC., SOCIETIES;
AUTHOR OF 'JOURNAL OF RESEARCHES DURING H. M. S. BEAGLE'S VOYAGE
ROUND THE WORLD.'

LONDON:
JOHN MURRAY, ALBEMARLE STREET.
1859.

The right of Translation is reserved.

Title page of the 1859 edition of Charles Darwin's On the Origin of Species. *The book, in which the English naturalist explains his theory of how evolution occurred, was an immediate success. However, it was not popular with people who believed that God created everything in the world all at one time. Darwin continued writing about his theory in several other books.* Library of Congress Prints and Photographs Division

published several books describing his travels and observations. One of the most famous was *On the Origin of Species*.

In 1868, the Russian chemist Dmitry Mendeleyev published *The Principles of Chemistry*. It contained what is now known as the periodic table, a chart in which the chemical elements are arranged in order of increasing weight. Mendeleyev's table was so accurate that he was able to point out gaps where undiscovered elements would belong on the table.

In the 1870s, the Scottish physicist James Clerk Maxwell developed a theory about electromagnetic radiation. Electromagnetic radiation includes radio waves, microwaves, visible light, ultraviolet light, X-rays, and gamma rays. Maxwell suggested that these forms of radiation all travel through space in wavelike patterns at the speed of light. In 1887, Heinrich Hertz developed a way of producing and receiving radio waves.

Perhaps one of the most significant scientific discoveries, in terms of its social influences, occurred in 1896. The French scientist Henri Becquerel left a uranium compound in a desk drawer. The drawer happened to contain a package of unused photographic plates. Later, when these plates were removed from their lightproof wrappers, Becquerel found them to be fogged. The only unusual thing near them had been the uranium compound. It was evident that the presence of the uranium had "exposed" the plates. This simple observation brought about another revolution in science.

Henri Becquerel. Photos.com/ Thinkstock

The fogging of the plates showed that they had been subjected to radiation.

The discovery of this type of radiation, which is produced by radioactivity, was followed by the discovery of the radioactive elements polonium and radium by Marie Curie and Pierre Curie. Two units of radioactivity measurement were named the becquerel and the curie. Radioactivity is now known to involve forces within the nuclei of atoms.

CHAPTER 5

THE 20TH CENTURY AND BEYOND

All of the discoveries that came before the 20th century opened unexpected doors and suggested fresh lines of investigation to new generations of scientists. The advance of science up to that point had produced many benefits for society—along with certain perils. In the process, it had presented countless new questions and challenges.

In increasing numbers, keen young minds answered the call to explore, examine, and experiment. The 20th century became the most profound time in the history of science. Striking new discoveries were announced at an accelerated pace. Scientists learned how to cure long-dreaded diseases, increase food production, create explosive powers beyond imagination, and send astronauts to the Moon and back. They also placed fathomless bodies of information, accumulated over hundreds of years, at the fingertips of everyone who had access to personal computers and the Internet.

20TH–CENTURY ADVANCES IN PHYSICS

Physicists originally thought that the amount of energy in the universe was constant. Energy was neither created nor destroyed; it was merely transformed. Similarly, the amount of matter was thought to be constant. A piece of iron could be ground into fine dust. The dust could be combined with oxygen to form iron oxides, but this was thought to be a change in form and shape, not a change in quantity.

It was Albert Einstein who proposed that perhaps it was not the amount of energy that was constant, nor the amount of matter, but the amount of the two combined that remained constant. In other words, if one really succeeded in the difficult process of destroying matter, then energy would be the result. If one succeeded in condensing energy, then matter would be the

German-born American physicist Albert Einstein. One of the greatest geniuses in the history of science, his theories led to new ways of thinking about time, space, matter, energy, gravity, and the universe. Encyclopædia Britannica, Inc.

result. These concepts are fundamental to the study of nuclear energy, called nuclear physics.

In 1934, the physicist Enrico Fermi accidentally split the nucleus of an atom when he bombarded uranium with neutrons. In 1939 the German scientists Otto Hahn, Lise Meitner, and Fritz Strassmann repeated some of Fermi's work and reported that nuclear fission had taken place. Three years later Fermi and his associates discovered that a nuclear chain reaction could be self-sustained. These discoveries led to the first nuclear weapons and reactors. In the decades following World War II, many uses were found for nuclear reactors, from nuclear-powered ships and submarines to nuclear power plants for generating electricity for public use. As powerful as the fission bomb (the atomic bomb) was, some scientists began to develop an even more deadly weapon—a nuclear fusion bomb (the hydrogen bomb), first tested in 1952.

In 1900, German physicist Max Planck proposed that electromagnetic energy was emitted and absorbed in small units, called quanta. This became known as the quantum theory. Einstein's explanation of the photoelectric effect in 1905 established the quantum theory of light. Many other scientists studied the structure of matter. It was through his

study of the deflection of nuclear particles as they passed through gold foil that Ernest Rutherford came to postulate a theory that the greatest mass of the atom was concentrated in a positively charged nucleus, around which the electrons revolved. Niels Bohr later developed a more complete theory of the structure of the atom and verified the quantum theory. The German scientist Werner Heisenberg contributed to the understanding of subatomic particles. In 1927, he stated that it was impossible to measure simultaneously both the position and the momentum (mass times velocity) of a subatomic body. This became known as the uncertainty principle.

DISCOVERIES IN GENETICS

Biologists continued to advance the genetics principles proposed by Mendel as they explored cell metabolism and reproduction. In 1953, James Watson and Francis Crick discovered that the DNA (deoxyribonucleic acid) molecule is in the shape of a double helix. DNA contains the master code of instructions for protein synthesis in the cell. Later research revealed the complex process by which the DNA code is read and

In 1953, England's Francis Crick and American James Watson joined forces to identify the double-helix structure of DNA, a discovery that helped explain how genetic information is passed along. Fritz Goro/ Time & Life Pictures/Getty Image

used by the cell to assemble amino acids into proteins by means of RNA (ribonucleic acid).

Scientists learned how to move a gene from one species and insert it into the DNA of another species, where it is replicated with the host DNA. This technique, a form of genetic engineering, made it possible to use bacteria to produce some types of human hormones, such as insulin and growth hormones. Genetic engineering has been applied in agriculture, medicine, and other fields. Genetically modified crops are widely grown in the United States and in other countries. One example is a type of genetically modified corn (maize) that contains a gene that produces a natural insecticide. DNA research has allowed scientists to map chromosomes and isolate the causes of some genetic anomalies. The first human trials of gene therapy began in 1990. In 2000, competing teams of researchers from private and public laboratories in the United States and Great Britain announced that they had completed the initial sequencing of the human genome.

THE TURN TOWARD OUTER SPACE

Many other scientific developments occurred in astronomy, the Earth sciences, and medicine. In the 1920s, some scientists began to propose that the universe was formed as a result of a violent explosion from a state of extremely high temperature and density. As evidence was discovered to support this so-called big bang theory, it eventually came to be accepted by the scientific community. The exploration of outer space began in 1957, first with unmanned space vehicles. Several countries subsequently launched unmanned satellites and probes that were sent through the solar system. Using space-based telescopes, free of

BIG BANG THEORY

The big bang theory is a general theory held by many astronomers that the universe may have originated about 13 to 14 billion years ago as the result of a violent explosion of some primordial mass; since then the universe has been expanding and evolving. One version of the theory states that the universe pulsates, expanding and contracting every 80 billion years.

atmospheric disturbances, scientists were able to see fainter and more-distant astronomical objects than before. Probes sent to the Moon and the planets have given scientists a better understanding of the nature and origins of those bodies.

Manned spaceflights began in 1961. On July 20, 1969, astronauts from the United States were the first to set foot on the Moon. In the 1970s, the United States developed the first reusable manned space vehicle, the space shuttle. At the end of the 20th century, the United States, Russia, Japan, Canada, and the European Space Agency cooperated to build the International Space Station in orbit around Earth. The first resident crew arrived at the station in 2000.

Apollo 11 *astronaut Edwin Aldrin (popularly known as Buzz), photographed July 20, 1969, during the first manned mission to the Moon's surface. Reflected in Aldrin's faceplate is the lunar module and astronaut Neil Armstrong, who took the picture.* NASA

HUBBLE SPACE TELESCOPE

The most sophisticated optical observatory ever placed into orbit around Earth is the Hubble Space Telescope (HST). Earth's atmosphere obscures ground-based astronomers' view of celestial objects by absorbing or distorting light rays from them. A telescope stationed in outer space is entirely above the atmosphere, receiving images of much greater brightness, clarity, and detail.

After the U.S. Congress had authorized its construction in 1977, the Hubble Space Telescope was built under the supervision of the National Aeronautics and Space Administration (NASA). It was named after Edwin Hubble, the foremost American astronomer of the 20th century. The HST was placed into orbit about 370 miles (600 kilometers) above Earth by the crew of the space shuttle *Discovery* on April 25, 1990. The HST is a large reflecting telescope whose mirror optics gather light from celestial objects and direct it into various recording instruments. It has a 94-inch (2.4-meter) primary mirror, a smaller secondary mirror, and recording instruments that can detect visible, ultraviolet, and infrared light.

About one month after launch, it became apparent that the HST's large primary mirror had been ground to the wrong shape owing to faulty testing procedures by the mirror's manufacturer. The resulting optical defect caused the mirror to produce fuzzy rather than sharp images. The HST also developed additional problems. On Dec. 2–13, 1993, a mission of the NASA space shuttle *Endeavour* sought to correct the telescope's optical system. The mission proved an unqualified success, and the HST soon began operating at its full potential, returning spectacular photographs of various cosmic phenomena.

Three subsequent space shuttle missions in 1997, 1999, and 2002 repaired the HST's gyroscopes and added new instruments, including a near-infrared spectrometer and a wide-field camera. The final space shuttle mission to service the HST installed a new camera and an ultraviolet spectrograph in 2009.

The HST's discoveries have revolutionized astronomy. Observations of Cepheid variables (a type of star whose observed light varies notably in intensity) in nearby

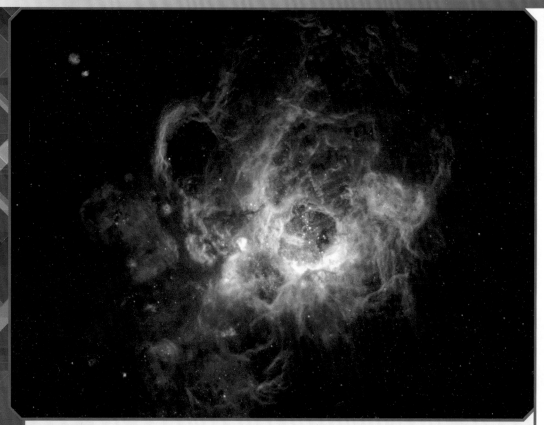

A Hubble Space Telescope image of NGC 604, a vast nebula (a cloud of gas and dust in space) that lies in a neighbouring galaxy located 2.7 million light-years from Earth. Hui Yang (University of Illinois) and NASA/ESA

galaxies allowed the first accurate determination of Hubble's constant, which is the rate of the universe's expansion. The HST photographed young stars with disks that will eventually become planetary systems. The Hubble Deep Field, a photograph of about 1,500 galaxies, revealed galactic evolution over nearly the entire history of the universe.

WEGENER'S CONTINENTAL DRIFT THEORY

In 1912 the German geologist and meteorologist Alfred Wegener proposed that the continents were once all one land mass, which he called Pangaea. For many years his continental drift theory was dismissed as highly speculative. Eventually evidence was accumulated in support of the theory, partly through the study of the phenomenon known as magnetic reversal. (Studies in the 1960s indicated that Earth's magnetic field repeatedly changes polarity at intervals of 100,000 to 50 million years.) The continental drift theory led to the concept of plate tectonics, which holds that Earth's outer layers are divided into moving plates and explains the existence of volcanoes and earthquakes. In 1935, the American seismologist Charles Richter devised the Richter scale for measuring the intensity of earthquakes.

MODERN MEDICINE

Many 20th-century medical developments were attributed to the invention of specialized devices. Shortly after the discovery of X-rays, physicians began to examine bone fractures

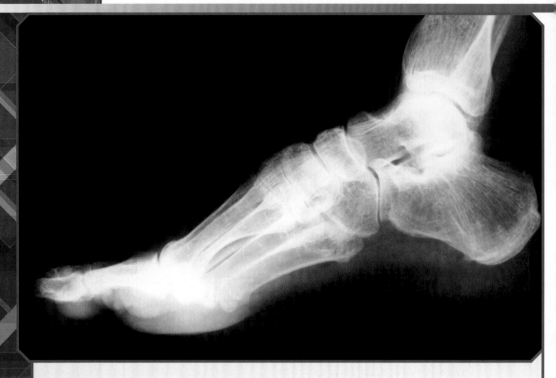

X-ray of a human foot. © Vadim Kozlovsky/Shutterstock.com

with X-ray machines. In 1912, U.S. chemist John Jacob Abel produced the first useful artificial kidney for use in the laboratory. It was to be followed by many other artificial devices to replace parts of the body, including ear drums, hips, heart valves, and the heart itself. The first dependable heart-lung machine was built in 1955. In 1967, Christiaan Barnard, a South African physician, performed the first successful heart transplant on a human. The heart recipient survived for 18 days. Important advances in the early 21st century included the development of prosthetic-limb technology, such as nerve biosensors to control movement.

Artificial insemination experiments were performed as early as 1780. In 1901, the Russian biologist Ilya Ivanovich Ivanov began artificial insemination of horses. The techniques were eventually used on humans, usually with couples having difficulty in conceiving children. In 1978, the first "test tube" baby was born in England as a result of in vitro fertilization of an egg cell and the implantation of the embryo in the mother's uterus.

Medical researchers had some success in the production of artificial blood, which may eventually eliminate the threat of

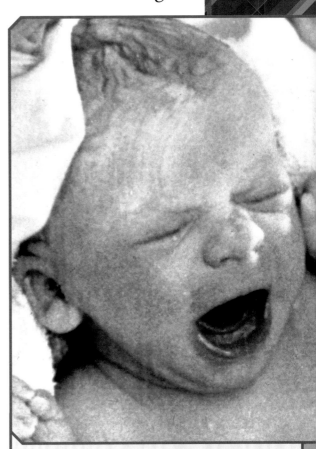

In 1977, a British physician removed an egg from the mother and fertilized it with sperm from the father, creating the first "test tube" baby conceived through the process of in vitro fertilization. The baby, Louise Joy Brown, pictured above on the day she was born, July 25, 1978, was thus the first human to be conceived outside of a woman's body. © AP Images

contracting diseases transmitted during blood transfusions. In the early 2000s, a high-tech bandage was introduced that promoted blood clotting and quickly stopped uncontrolled bleeding from a wound.

INFORMATION TECHNOLOGY

Many scientific advances would never have been made without the use of computers. Thus, the invention of electronic computers was among the most significant achievements of the 20th century. The first electronic digital computers were built in the 1940s. The reduction in size and increase in speed of computers were spurred by the invention of the transistor in the late 1940s and the integrated circuit in the late 1950s. The first personal computers became widely available after the introduction of random-access memory chips and microprocessors in the early 1970s. Soon a larger variety of computer programs were developed as commercial products. The Internet, whose origins date to the 1960s, had very limited use by the general public until the development of the World Wide Web in the early 1990s. In the early 21st century, handheld computer devices with access to the World Wide Web

The Harvard Mark I, an electromechanical computer designed by American mathematician Howard Aiken, was more than 50 feet (15 meters) long and contained some 750,000 components. It was used to make ballistics calculations during World War II. IBM Archives

were developed and were soon incorporated with cellular telephones.

One advanced area of computer research is the field of artificial intelligence. Artificial intelligence has many potential applications in robotics, communications, and other fields.

SCIENTIFIC COMMUNICATION

Scientists frequently cooperate with other scientists in their research. Cooperative

efforts may involve scientists from many different countries. Another way in which scientists share their research is by attending local, national, or international conferences. Conferences are periodic meetings in which scientists formally or informally present their research and opinions. Conferences provide scientists with immediate feedback on their work. Many historic scientific breakthroughs have been presented to the scientific community at such conferences. Consequently, many scientists attend conferences to follow scientific developments and share methods, results, and ideas with other researchers. In addition to attending conferences, many scientists regularly correspond with one another. Some of these letters have become historic documents.

Researchers may also write formal papers describing their experimental procedures, hypotheses, results, and conclusions. These papers may be submitted to a science academy or association for publication. Such organizations help to foster support and communication among scientists. Even if the paper is not selected for publication, it serves as written documentation of the work and enables other scientists to replicate or evaluate the experiment.

Nearly every scientific advancement made today is published in some form of scientific literature. Some journals are devoted to an entire field, such as biology, while others focus on research in a highly specialized area, such as cetaceans (whales, dolphins, and porpoises). A journal may be interdisciplinary, or it may concentrate on a specific theme such as environmental conservation.

FUNDING AND AWARDS

Scientific research can be extremely expensive, especially when it involves the use of costly equipment. Research may be funded by governments, industries, foundations, or universities. In the United States, the federal government sponsors many projects in the area of national defense and space exploration. In 1950, Congress passed an act that established the National Science Foundation. The purpose of this independent federal agency is to develop a national science policy and to support basic scientific research and education. Other foundations, such as the National Heart Association and the American Cancer Society, are devoted to research concerning human health.

Scientific research is also supported by the private sector. Industries frequently employ scientists, especially those who work in the applied sciences. These scientists are involved in the development of industrial or commercial processes and products. Colleges and universities support scientific research by offering professorships. As professors, scientists usually divide their time between their individual research and teaching. In this way, their students have the opportunity to observe the scientific process firsthand. Universities may specialize in various fields, and they are frequently judged on the basis of the accomplishments

The 2013 Nobel Prize Award Ceremony with the Swedish royal family onstage, Stockholm, Sweden. Pascal Le Segretain/Getty Images

of their professors and scientists. Scientists who publish, therefore, bring prestige to their college or university.

Scientists are often awarded for their contribution to science. Perhaps the most well-known award is the Nobel Prize, a yearly recognition of the leaders within the fields of physics, chemistry, physiology (or medicine), literature, and peace. The award was established by Alfred Nobel, a Swedish chemist and the inventor of dynamite. In 1968, an economics prize was added. The winners of the Nobel Prize receive money, a gold medal, and a diploma. The award honors the most significant and outstanding achievements in each field. In keeping with Nobel's will, the Royal Swedish Academy considers persons of any nationality as eligible for the award.

HIGGS BOSON: THE GOD PARTICLE

In physics, a recent issue of notable interest is the Higgs boson particle, or Higgs particle. This hypothetical particle of mass may be the carrier particle, or boson, of the so-called Higgs field. The Higgs field theoretically permeates space, affecting all subatomic particles. The field and the particle—named after Peter

Higgs, one of the physicists who in 1964 proposed it—offer a hypothesis for the origin of mass that can be tested.

In popular culture, the Higgs boson is often called the "God particle." Nobel physicist Leon Lederman's popular science book *The God Particle: If the Universe Is the Answer, What Is the Question?* was published in 1993. Lederman asserted that the discovery of the particle is crucial to a final understanding of the structure of matter.

The Higgs field is different from other fundamental fields (such as the electromagnetic field) that underlie the basic forces between particles. First, it has magnitude but no direction; this implies that the Higgs boson has a spin of zero, unlike the carriers of the force fields, which do have spin. Second, the Higgs field has the unusual property that its energy is higher when the field is zero than when it is nonzero. The hypothesis for how the Higgs field and Higgs boson give rise to mass has important implications concerning the way fundamental physical forces relate to each and in the development of the universe in the aftermath of its origin in the big bang.

Evidence has suggested the possibility that there is more than one type of Higgs boson.

British physicist Peter Higgs at the opening of a multimedia exhibit on the Higgs boson, London, 2013. Peter Macdiarmid/Getty Images

On July 4, 2012, scientists announced they had detected an interesting signal that was likely from a Higgs boson with a mass of 125–126 gigaelectron volts (billion electron volts). Further data confirming those observations were announced in March 2013. Higgs and Belgian physicist François Englert (who had also proposed the Higgs mechanism) shared the 2013 Nobel Prize in Physics.

CONCLUSION

The underlying objective of much scientific research, especially in applied science, is to improve people's lives. Pessimists point out, though, that many scientific discoveries have caused harm. For example, certain drug compounds that help cure illnesses have been found to cause fatal side effects. The first scientists to study the nucleus of the atom never imagined that their work would lead to the making of hydrogen bombs. During the 20th century, numerous good uses were found for asbestos, such as building insulation—until it was proved to cause cancer. The U.S. Environmental Protection Agency in 1989 ordered asbestos to be phased out of construction. The Internet and computer technology are extremely versatile tools that have given everyone powers that were undreamed of only a generation ago. These tools, however, can also be exploited by criminals and terrorists.

Scientists cannot let setbacks and wrongdoing undermine their efforts. Alfred Nobel, one of the most famous scientists of all time, was a prolific inventor who held some 350 patents and became very wealthy. His best-known invention? Dynamite. A French newspaper branded him "the merchant of death" who "became rich by finding ways to kill more people faster than ever before." Ashamed, Nobel left most of his fortune to fund the annual Nobel Prizes. They encourage and reward efforts in science, literature, and the pursuit of world peace.

The historic quest for new discoveries goes on in many different fields. Science is a continuing story. Its coming chapters will undoubtedly hold surprises for everyone.

GLOSSARY

amino acids Acids that are key components of proteins; they are especially important to the diet.

artificial insemination Achieving pregnancy by an artificial means.

artificial intelligence Computerized simulation of human intelligence.

ballistics Study of projectiles in flight.

celestial Pertaining to the Sun, Moon, stars, and other heavenly objects.

genetics Biological science that studies heredity.

genome An organism's genetic material.

Ice Age Period of history noted for excessively low temperatures, resulting in massive glaciers.

interdisciplinary Describes studies combining two or more branches, or disciplines, of science.

logarithm The power to which a base number must be raised to yield a specified number.

malleable Capable of being reshaped.

memory chip Small computer part for storing great quantities of digital information.

metabolism Process of chemical change that produces energy in the human body.

microbiology Study of microscopic life forms.

microprocessor Miniaturized electronic circuit that processes instructions and data in a computer.

optics Study of light and its properties.

ozone Form of oxygen that pollutes Earth's lower atmosphere but absorbs harmful solar rays in the upper atmosphere.

polarity Either of two opposite states that occur in certain phenomena, such as electricity (positive or negative poles) and magnetism (north or south poles).

power grid Network of transmission lines for delivering electric power.

prosthetic Pertaining to an artificial body part.

protein Complex natural substance consisting of amino acids and multiple chemical elements.

radiation Emission of energy in the form of waves or particles.

seismologist Scientist who studies earthquakes.

smelting Process of refining or separating pure metals.

subatomic Relating to particles smaller than atoms.

synthetic Produced artificially by chemical processes.

vaccination Introducing a substance in the body to develop an immunity.

FOR MORE INFORMATION

American Association for the Advancement
    of Science
1200 New York Avenue NW
Washington, DC 20005
(202) 326-6400
Website: http://www.aaas.org
Founded in 1848, the association is the
    "world's largest general-science society"
    and is affiliated with more than 260 sci-
    entific organizations. Founded in 1880, it
    publishes *Science* magazine.

American Museum of Natural History
Central Park West at 79th Street
New York, NY 10024-5192
(212) 769-5100
Website: http://www.amnh.org
An internationally prominent scientific
    and cultural museum that was founded
    in 1869. Its mission is to discover,
    interpret, and disseminate informa-
    tion about human cultures, the natural
    world, and the universe through scien-
    tific research, educational programs,
    and exhibitions.

Canada Science and Technology Museum
1867 Saint Laurent Boulevard
Ottawa, ON K1G 5A3
Canada
(613) 991-3044
(866) 442-4416
Website: http://www.sciencetech.technomuses
.ca/English/index.cfm
The largest museum of its kind in Canada offers vast collections, permanent and temporary exhibits, workshops and demonstrations, school programs, conferences, and lectures.

The Field Museum
1400 S. Lake Shore Drive
Chicago, IL 60605-2496
(312) 922-9410
Website: http://fieldmuseum.org
Founded in 1893, the museum is noted for its permanent collections and traveling exhibitions pertaining to multiple facets of natural and cultural history and science.

National Science Foundation
4201 Wilson Boulevard
Arlington, VA 22230
(703) 292-5111, (800) 877-8339
Website: http://www.nsf.gov

The National Science Foundation is a federal agency created by Congress in 1950. It promotes science and public welfare largely through research grants to universities and colleges.

Smithsonian Institution
1000 Jefferson Drive SW
Washington, DC 20004
(202) 633-1000
Website: http://www.si.edu
The institution's website contains educational resources for students in the categories of "Science & Nature," "History & Culture," and others.

WEBSITES

Because of the changing nature of Internet links, Rosen Publishing has developed an online list of websites related to the subject of this book. This site is updated regularly. Please use this link to access the list:

http://www.rosenlinks.com/SCI/Hist

FOR FURTHER READING

Bryson, Bill. *A Really Short History of Nearly Everything*. New York, NY: Delacorte Books (Random House), 2009.

Concise History of Science & Invention: An Illustrated Time Line. Washington, DC: National Geographic, 2009.

Dinwiddie, Robert, et al. *Science: The Definitive Visual Guide*. New York, NY: DK Publishing, 2011.

Jackson, Tom. *Science* (DK Eyewitness Books). New York, NY: DK Publishing, 2011.

Krull, Kathleen, and Kathryn Hewitt. *Lives of the Scientists: Experiments, Explosions (and What the Neighbors Thought)*. Boston, MA: Harcourt Children's Books, 2013.

Mullins, Lisa. *Science in the Renaissance* (Renaissance World). New York, NY: Crabtree Publishing, 2009.

Rooney, Anne. *The History of Medicine* (The History of Science). New York, NY: Rosen Publishing, 2012.

Smithsonian Timelines of Science. New York, NY: DK Publishing, 2013.

Steele, Philip. *Isaac Newton: The Scientist Who Changed Everything*. Washington, DC: National Geographic Children's Books, 2013.

INDEX